NORWICH

Edited by Michelle Warrington

First published in Great Britain in 1998 by
POETRY NOW YOUNG WRITERS
1-2 Wainman Road, Woodston,
Peterborough, PE2 7BU
Telephone (01733) 230748

HB ISBN 0 75430 209 1
SB ISBN 0 75430 210 5

FOREWORD

With over 63,000 entries for this year's Cosmic competition, it has proved to be our most demanding editing year to date.

We were, however, helped immensely by the fantastic standard of entries we received, and, on behalf of the Young Writers team, thank you.

The Cosmic series is a tremendous reflection on the writing abilities of 8-11 year old children, and the teachers who have encouraged them must take a great deal of credit.

We hope that you enjoy reading *Cosmic Norwich* and that you are impressed with the variety of poems and style with which they are written, giving an insight into the minds of young children and what they think about the world today.

CONTENTS

THE POEMS

BANG!

Racing through the solar system,
At the speed of light,
Looking at the constellations,
The stars, they are so bright!

Going past Jupiter,
Seeing the red spot,
Going past Venus,
Boy, that looks hot!

As we see Mars,
Redder than ever,
We suddenly feel,
Light as a feather.

Gravity leaks in,
We're trying to stop it,
Disaster strikes,
And bang goes the rocket!

Owen Gregory (11)

STARS IN SPACE

I watch the stars
every night
I watch them gleam
very bright
Hovering around the moon
I have to go to bed
very soon
Every planet has gone
to sleep
Except Jupiter
the biggest one
Who's watching over everyone.

Samuel Mardell (9)
Bunwell CP School

THE AUTUMN DAY

The wind blows my hair
The leaves blow my face
When I spade the leaves up
Then the wind blows them off.

I'm cold
It's quiet everywhere
A conker falls in the leaves.

I hear the leaves crunch
I pick a leaf
It falls to pieces in my hand
Leaves fall from the tree.

Kirsty Thorpe (9)
Bunwell CP School

AUTUMN GARDEN

There's a breeze
in the garden,
and the trees are bare,
because their leaves
are everywhere,
noisy whistling
crinkling leaves,
colours of leaves
in the breeze.
There's a rustling sound
when they come down
green, yellow, red
and golden brown.

Chloë Riley (8)
Bunwell CP School

CONKER SHELL

Falling from the tree
comes a conker
plain and round,
hard and brown,
brown and shiny,
nice and brown,
fresh from the conker shell.

Big and small
different sizes too
falling off the conker tree.

Ashley Smith (8)
Bunwell CP School

THE CONKER

A conker fell from the conker tree
      in the autumn breeze.

It fell with a clash and a bang
      into the wet grass.

The conker fell out of the prickly case
      brown and very beautiful.

The conker buried itself under the wet grass
      where feet passed.

A little boy came and found the conker
      and then went home.

Nichaela Rudge (9)
Bunwell CP School

DO COME SEE THE LEAVES

When
the trees
do go
to bed
the leaves
of theirs
they do
shed.
Light as
the air
they go
down,
green,
yellow,
red
and
golden
brown.
To the ground.
Black
grey
and brown.
They
are
no
more.
Oh, do come
see
the leaves.

Jessica Daw (9)
Bunwell CP School

CONKERS

Conkers are shiny
brown and lovely
they grow on trees
and fall on
the green grass.
Conkers grow in their
prickly shells
on trees near churches.
Children collect them
and keep them.

Conkers are little jewels.

Sarah Crutchlow (9)
Bunwell CP School

LEAVES

Oh lovely leaves
falling from the trees
red, yellow and brown.

Leaves swirling
in the air,
ready to crumble.

How many
      can you
            catch?

Jenny Billin (8)
Bunwell CP School

THE ALTO OF KAD

Who or what is the Alto of Kad
has he got a mum has he got a dad,
                    the Alto of Kad?
Is he happy, sad,
angry
            or mad
                    the Alto of Kad?
Can he take away, can he divide
multiply
            or can he add
                    the Alto of Kad?
Is he good or is he bad
                    the Alto of Kad?
Is he young or is
he an old
            lad
                    the Alto of Kad?
Someone knows who or what
is the Alto of Kad.

Richard Howlett (9)
Bunwell CP School

THE LIN OF SUNIN

Who or what is
  the Lin of Sunin?
Does he eat from a pot
or a tin
  the Lin of Sunin?

Where does he live
in a cottage, a house
or a bin,
  the Lin of Sunin?

Does he race and lose
or win
  the Lin of Sunin?

Nobody knows
  the Lin of Sunin?

Andrew Driver (9)
Bunwell CP School

THE THING OF ING

Who, why or what is the Thing of Ing?
Maybe it's rich or poor
        or a king
                The Thing of Ing
Does he wear a necklace, earrings
        or a ring?
                The Thing of Ing
Is he happy or sad, does he like
to shout
        or sing?
                The Thing of Ing
Does he play with yo-yos
        or on a swing?
                The Thing of Ing
At bring and buy sales
Does he buy
        or bring?
                The Thing of Ing
Does somebody or nobody
or something
        know
                The Thing of Ing?

Henri Loombe-Temple (9)
Bunwell CP School

THE I DUNNO WHAT

Who or why or what is
             The I Dunno
             What
Does he play in the garden or swing on
the swing
             The I Dunno
             What
Does he sleep on a mat or in a cot
             The I Dunno
             What
Does he wear shorts with stripes or a dot
             The I Dunno
             What.

Emma Browes (9)
Bunwell CP School

THE JUNGLE

The trees reach for the sun,
Monkeys swinging by their tails,
Tigers crawling on the damp soil,
Ready to pounce on their unlucky prey.
Crocodiles' heads poking just out of the swamp pool.
Frogs leaping slowly away from the slithering snakes,
Gorillas basking in the trees in the hot humid sun,
Wood rotting and smelling rancid,
Birds twittering in the sky,
Their colours dazzling you,
Mist falls over the dark forest in the night,
Cleared by the howling, screaming wind,
Then pitch black and silence but for the hissing of the snakes.
Heavy rain arrives in the morning,
The animals hide till it stops,
That is the jungle.

Andrew Muir (10)
Colman Middle School

THE JUNGLE

Hot and humid I trek through the jungle,
Panting panthers sprinting from danger,
They pant and pant desperate for water,
Suddenly a tiger appears from the emerald bushes,
I run and run as far as possible,
Then a loud roar of thunder can be heard,
And the animals scatter for shelter,
A monkey groaning, a bird panicking
The jungle is very noisy.

The monsoon is setting in throughout the jungle,
You can hear dripping and gushing,
I walk on till I come to a mango tree,
The tropical fruit tastes juicy,
A parrot swoops over,
Its feathers are beautiful and very colourful,
It makes a screeching sound,
I go past swinging monkeys and sloppy mud,
The animals are happy,
The jungle has been very dry and now there's a lot
                                    of rain water.

Kate Brown (9)
Colman Middle School

THE JUNGLE

The ground is covered with dark sticky mud,
Tall skinny trees shade the earth.
I'm surrounded by brightly coloured plants and flowers.
Crocodiles and alligators are bathing in the swamps,
Snakes coil themselves round the tree trunks,
Cheeky monkeys swing from branch to branch,
Tigers are watching me with sharp eyes from a distance.
I am feeling very sore from mosquito bites,
There's an awful smell of rotting wood.
Water from the waterfall is scrambling over the rocks
Whooshing as it goes.
The squawking parrots in the treetops are getting annoying now.
The sky is clouding over,
Crash!
Flash!
We're having a thunder storm,
Oh no! The river is overflowing,
Everywhere is in complete chaos.

Sally Thirkettle (10)
Colman Middle School

THE JUNGLE

It's hot and humid in the jungle,
Dangerous predators prowl around,
Hunting at night,
Resting all day.
Tall dark trees are still,
All day and night.
Step by step,
I stride through a swamp,
Muddy and wet.
I see a waterfall,
Clean water falls from it,
It looks wonderful.
A tiger roars,
It sounds close,
I run,
I run to the campsite,
We all fall asleep,
Our busy day has ended.

Jimmy Barnard (10)
Colman Middle School

In The Jungle

Deep in the jungle
There are tigers growling
Birds are singing
Snakes are wrapping themselves around logs
Chattering monkeys swinging to and fro
There are lots of insects swarming around
I think there's going to be a storm
So I'll hide under a tree with the centipede and worm
The toads are happy I wonder why
Could there be a swamp nearby?
Yes! I see a crocodile
Hiding like the bark of a tree for a while
His eyes are closed so I know he cannot see me
The storm has eased so I can carry on my journey
My boots are all muddy
I feel wet and damp
I feel as if I have miles to tramp
But then I see a waterfall
Are there fish in it I wonder?
I'm not lost after all
It is getting gloomy and dark now
I hear a tiger I wonder if he's nearby
But now I can hear wooing and rustling
I am very hungry
I wish I could go home
So I'll sit by a tree and go to sleep.

Natasha Morgan (10)
Colman Middle School

JUNGLE

I was walking through the jungle
The flowers were in bloom
The birds were whistling in the breeze
Swooping at others who dare enter their territory.
I looked upon my dirty brown shoes
And saw a long green snake
Slithering over my feet.
There were many species of animal
And billions of bugs
Most bugs were flies.
A lizard climbed up the tree
It was a salamander lizard
There was a swamp
It had glaring eyes
The eyes of crocodiles.
A head of a tiger is peeking through the long grass
Waiting to pounce.
A poisonous frog creeps in the weeds
And a gorilla eats greedily.
A panda chews a bamboo shoot.

Michael Weavers (9)
Colman Middle School

THE JUNGLE

There are tigers ready to pounce
The snake trying to feed.
I can hear the mud squishing in my wellies,
I can hear the drip, dripping of the leaves.
I am speaking to myself to try and keep me jolly
But then someone or something is speaking back to me
A parrot laughed.

I can smell the fruit
I am so hot.
The smell of the jungle reeks!
I sat under the tree
I went to the river to get a drink.
A leopard jumped out of the tree
I thought it was after me but it was
After the snake.

Kelly Everett (9)
Colman Middle School

THE JUNGLE

I walked into the jungle and explored
It was full of noises.
The flowers were big and long spreading around the place
The rivers were flowing over for animals to drink!
Monkeys swing everywhere
People try to shoot
Animal traps are spreading
Snakes hissing all around.
Fresh food for them to eat
Parrots flying away from danger
Crocodiles swimming fast
Birds singing everywhere
Tigers growling for food
Toads hopping around the place.

Zoe Leigh Whitworth (10)
Colman Middle School

THE JUNGLE

My plane has crashed
In the middle of a dark jungle,
Steam and mist makes it hard to see,
Howling monkeys nearly deafen me,
Mosquitoes sting me,
Hungry tigers try to eat me,
Flies zip around me,
And I hit them away.
Moths frighten me,
The fresh smell of fruit
Makes me pick a mango from a tree.
A native finds me,
To take me to his territory.
I cannot understand him,
I run away,
Run back to the plane,
Fix it,
And fly away home
To my family . . . *safely!*

Genevieve Beavan (10)
Colman Middle School

THE JUNGLE

There were animals
And trees and funny shaped leaves
There were big swamps
The weather was hot
So I was sweating.
I could hear birds singing
It was scary.
Thunder flashed
With a loud bang
There were long snakes
I could see a waterfall
And a crocodile.
There was green grass everywhere
And lovely flowers.
I could hear howling
I could see lovely colours
In the jungle.

Deanne Tye (9)
Colman Middle School

THE JUNGLE

Sun shining just above me
The green long trees
Monkeys swinging from tree to tree
The waterfalls are blue
The animals all around me
Birds above me high in the sky
Beautiful flowers
Mud on the ground
Insects on the mud
Hunters with their guns
Bang bang! Mist in the sky
Koalas up in the trees
Food on the floor
Food on the trees.

Fay King (9)
Colman Middle School

THE JUNGLE

There was heavy rain pouring down
I could hear whooping from the monkeys and
Growling from the tigers.
I felt frightened, I felt scared and I felt lonely.
I could see water pouring from waterfalls,
Lots of very colourful plants
Dirty and muddy swamps, crystal clear rivers,
Exotic fruits, mosquitoes, frogs leaping and leeches
There were insects bites all over me,
Smells of rotten wood and the sweet flowers.
It felt very lonely and desolate.

Joseph Bell (10)
Colman Middle School

JUNGLE

I heard a noise in the jungle
Then I saw it was a tiger!
Suddenly it pounced straight at me.
Also snakes swirling around my feet,
Hissing
Then I saw monkeys swing from tree to tree
Suddenly I heard another noise
Then I saw a pied panda and its baby
Sitting in the treetops.

Stacey Larnder (10)
Colman Middle School

JUNGLE

In the jungle tigers are growling
Colourful birds are singing
Crocodiles swimming in the swamps
Sweat drips down my face
Pitter patter of rain falling on the ground
Up in the air monkeys swing in the trees.

Kim Louise Tompson (9)
Colman Middle School

TRAVELLING IN TIME

The clock was ticking on,
I was travelling in time.
As I travelled the colours were blurred,
My head was swirling,
I was whirling,
It was a strong sensation,
As though I was on a roller-coaster.
I was spinning around faster and faster,
The walls were closing in on me,
When all of a sudden there was a flash of light,
And everything went black,
I found myself in my bed,
And everything went dead.

Hannah Mason (10)
Falcon Middle School

TIME

One day when I was walking,
I started talking,
When I said about my past,
I was disappearing really fast.

As I travelled through time
I felt really ill,
I felt very much like jelly,
And it was as if I had a hole,
Right through my belly.

As I travelled back in time,
I felt dizzy in my mind,
As I reached my past,
I hoped this feeling wouldn't last.

Kayleigh Freezer (9)
Falcon Middle School

THE JOURNEY THROUGH TIME

I always get nervous when travelling through time,
Every day I find new places.
I go to 20 BC and have some tea,
And crack some unsolved cases.

My stomach gets knotted
My head starts to spin,
And before I know it
I'm in a Roman bin.

People think I'm weird
When I tell them where I've been
But I don't care one bit
Because I know what I've seen.

Thomas Greenwood (10)
Falcon Middle School

THE COLOUR OF TIME

Colours are curling,
My brain is whirling.
The place is wonderful,
This view is beautiful.
Suddenly the sight went black,
There was a deafening crack.
Time dimensions all around,
After that I leapt from the ground.
I got stuck in a bubble
I knew it meant trouble.
Someone's coming along with a pin,
Good! He only gave me a grin.
But . . . bang,
Colours are curling,
My brain really is whirling.
But . . . here we go again
        and again
                and again.

Samantha Gooda (10)
Falcon Middle School

TRAVELLING THROUGH TIME

In May I walked through a brick wall,
I was swirling round and round.
A bunch of wild flowers blew up at me,
There were daffodils and daisies,
All smelling good and strong.
Now buttercups came up and everything was yellow
And at this point I caught a roller-coaster,
It took me to a world of sand and sea,
There were mermaids and dolphins and lots of starfish.
The sand was smooth,
The sea was calm,
The mermaids and dolphins were diving
In and out for playtime fun.
The starfish were laying as still as a startled space ranger.
I thought I'd had too much excitement,
So I jumped back on the roller-coaster,
Went back through the wall,
I ended up in my bedroom on the floor,
With a thumping headache,
Then I knew that I had fallen out of bed.

Stacey Rivett (9)
Falcon Middle School

TRAVELLING IN TIME

I'm going through the freezing fridge,
My heart is in my throat.
Past the yoghurts, past the milk,
Oops I've landed in some yolk!

I feel like I'm in a fantasy world,
With circles all around me.
I'm going through a weirdo stage,
In which I'm unable to see.

Romans, Greeks that's all I need,
Now I've turned into a weed.
What's happening I don't know,
I can't stay long . . . here I go.

Jennie Stewart (10)
Falcon Middle School

TIME TRAVEL

I feel like a little bird who's still asleep in bed,
My stomach feels all whirly and my feet are above my head,
I feel like a puff of wind floating in the sky,
I feel like a little wren learning how to fly.

I see below me fields of many coloured greens,
I think that I am going through a massive washing machine
After that I think I'm a prawn swimming in the sea.
I look at all those people who would like to eat me.

Tudors, Greeks, that's all I need,
Now I've turned into a seed.
Will they plant me in the ground?
At least when I sprout I'll be found.

Alishia Douce (10)
Falcon Middle School

TIME

In a time machine I go,
Entering a strange new world,
Of colours, and yet of none,
Silly things of such fun,
Through nooks, crannies, doorways, alleys,
To heaven and a world of mortals,
To past, present and future tense,
The movement creating the sixth new sense.
A strange feeling it was to me
Non-existent, as real as can be
60 million years fly by
A long time to you and I
But a drop in deepest ocean
The Sea of Time.

Lewis Robbins (9)
Falcon Middle School

TIME TRAVELLING

When you travel through time
It feels like you're walking through the air.
In front is an endless spiral
Of black and white stripes.
You hear the sound of crying wolves.
To travel through time
You have to go under the bed
You imagine illusions of the weirdest things
Like dogs with three heads and horses running with fear.
You see Hades, God of the underworld
You see Greeks and Romans having a battle.
After that a ship flies by
With trolls on board,
And monsters on the deck.
It all goes black
You're going quite fast and *bang!*
It's over.

Antony Pearce (9)
Falcon Middle School

THE JOURNEY THROUGH TIME

I'm twisting and twirling,
The colours are swirling,
The clocks ticking by,
The calendars fly.
There's a strange sensation in the air,
I know this feeling must be rare.
Romans, Greeks, when will it end?
There's a hole in time I have to mend.
I'm feeling sick, I'm feeling ill,
There are Vikings out there and they're ready to kill.
Hang on a minute I'm slowing down,
Queen Elizabeth's about to be crowned.
I'm twisting and twirling,
The colours are swirling,
And I'm home.

Jessica French (9)
Falcon Middle School

TIME AT NIGHT

There was a smart sensation in the air,
I began to twist and twirl.
Colours began to spin and fade,
And stars were shining up above.
My window flew open,
And I floated out into the sky.
Over the city and through the clouds,
Twisting and turning past the chimneys.
Suddenly the view changed,
Houses disappeared and so did the park.
Up came new buildings as tall as can be,
A city of neon lights.
Casinos, cinemas and theme parks everywhere.
It looked like Los Angeles,
But bigger and better.
At that time I realised,
I was in the future!
What an experience,
Seeing your city 100 years later.
I started slowing down,
Just drifting through the sky.
Everything stopped,
And I found myself once again.

Hannah Ward (10)
Falcon Middle School

TIME

Spinning, twirling, round and round,
Both my feet lift off the ground.
Upside down, inside out,
What can this be all about?

I feel a cold wind on my face,
That's when I realise I've travelled through space.
What is this place? Nobody knows.
Is it where lost property goes?

I feel so scared but yet such joy,
I've found at last my long lost toy.
I never thought I'd get it back,
All at once I sense the black.

Spinning, twirling, round and round,
Both my feet lift off the ground.
Upside down, inside out,
I know what this is all about.

Nicola Brown (9)
Falcon Middle School

TRAVELLING IN A TIME MACHINE

When you are in a time machine
It feels like you're in space.
You hear a little tingling sound
It's a very big case.
For Superman,
Batman or
Robin.
I'm not quite sure
But anyway I don't care.
I'm just carrying on at a great speed
About 50 miles per millisecond I think.
But I'm dreading the time
When I feel myself fall.
Plunging,
Plunging,
Plunging,
Bang!
What was that I said?
I found myself lying in bed.
I think it's over
Yes, it is.

Martin Clarke (9)
Falcon Middle School

A TIME TRAVEL TRIP

When I was in a time machine
I felt really funny,
I thought I was a hungry fox
Chasing a very large bunny.
When I had seen a dinosaur
And felt like a volcano,
I knew that was in the past
Where everyone's a foe.
Next I felt like Mr Bean
Doing lots of strange things,
And yet I felt just like a fly
But with robotic wings.
When I was looking at the sky
A very big starfish caught my eye,
It was strange that it had come from the deep
I really didn't know why.
But when I found I was back home
I cried out with joy,
But when someone stole my time machine
My shout was, 'I'll get that boy.'

Andrew Hardman (9)
Falcon Middle School

THE WONDERS OF TIME TRAVEL!

Curling, whirling, swirling
Down a tube.
Curling, whirling, swirling
Into space.
Curling, whirling, swirling
What a sight.
Curling, whirling, swirling
Now what's that?
Curling, whirling, swirling
It's a beast.
Curling, whirling, swirling
With sharpened tooth.
Curling, whirling, swirling
Now it's gone.
Curling, whirling, swirling
Relief's mine.
Curling, whirling, swirling
All is calm.
No more curling, no more whirling
No more swirling.

Thomas Wozniakowski (9)
Falcon Middle School

TRAVELLING THROUGH TIME

When you travel through time,
It feels like you are riding on a skateboard sideways.
You hear some faint music
Like someone playing a violin, a drum and a piano.
You see some people and then they fade away.
You hear people counting numbers, reading stories and newspapers,
You hear the music again,
You feel your head is spinning round and round
And you come to land with a big bump.

Laura Broome (9)
Falcon Middle School

TIME

Travelling through time
You see everybody,
Victorians, Greeks, even mummies.

When I looked round,
It went black and white
I could not see a single thing.

I heard a noise,
A very funny sort of sound
It went like this . . . *boosshh boosshh.*

Suddenly I felt ill,
I felt really sick.
I heard somebody say, 'How are you?'
And I fainted.

Charlotte Ellis (9)
Falcon Middle School

A VERY FRIENDLY ALIEN

Hello Mr Alien
Sitting in your ship
Your body is green
But red is your lip.

I can't really see you
You're stuck in a tree
Struggling to get out
While staring at me.

Hello Mr Alien
Though I've said it before
You've only had a little food
And wishing for more.

I don't believe this alien
I'm reading your mind
You're looking for some treasure
That you just can't find.

Gold glimmering
Shining in your eye
Sorry that can't be true
Please don't give a sigh.

Bye, bye Mr Alien
Sad to see you go
I'll come tomorrow to see you
And give you a big blue bow.

Hannah Cott (9)
Kenninghall CP School

COSMIC COLOURS

Cosmic is red, red as Mars other colours too
Cosmic is yellow, green maybe purple too
Cosmic is gold, silver, *wow!*
Cosmic is black, white and grey
Cosmic is brown, cream and pink do you really think?
Cosmic is orange, ginger too
Cosmic is weird and wonderful oooh!
Cosmic is magic it disappears
Cosmic is hot, hot as the sun.
Cosmic is space, everything rolled into one.

Oliver Wilson (8)
Kenninghall CP School

PET DOG JESSY

J essy is cuddly, very cuddly
E ating very fast
S ipping up the water
S loppy dog in my house
Y apping all day long.

Amy Easton (8)
Kenninghall CP School

BONES

Under the ground
Just waiting to be found
Bones are rattling
Clattering and chattering
Full of excitement
But they are not going to be found
In the ground
Until fifty million years later.

James Regan (9)
Kenninghall CP School

PEOPLE

Bottoms out, heads up high
See the people walking by
Lovely people far and near
Dogs scurrying everywhere
Hear the sound that trees make
Children playing on garden gates
See the shadows that people make
See the baker baking cakes.

Leah Mann (9)
Larkman Middle School

THE FLICKERING

In the distance, I can see little dots flickering
sunlight, peeping through the tall tree trunks
like millions of tiny glow-worms
looking from the sky so high.

Katrina Jane Purdy (10)
Larkman Middle School

THE UPS AND DOWNS OF THE YORKSHIRE DALES

When we climb so really high
It makes you want to really fly.
But what would we do
When the wind really blew?
What about flying when it really snowed?
I think I would rather be on the ground,
Where Nanny and Grandad would make sure I was found.
I always made sure of my boots, gloves and hat
And made sure I had loads of food in my back pack.
I hope you like sheep, because they always peep,
I hope you like rabbits, because there were hundreds to see;
Dead ones, baby ones, rotten ones, from morning till tea,
And talking about food,
The best place was the pub,
I ate my curry, and it was lovely grub.
When we walked we used to talk
About the wonderful scenery,
I'd love to live there all my life,
But I think I'll stick to Norwich!

Georgiana Simmons (10)
Larkman Middle School

WALLS AND FALLS

Walls and falls are everywhere,
People screaming far and near.
Cannonballs coming from high up there,
Floods and mud are mixing where,
People dropping everywhere,
Hear the bangs every day,
Blue skies are floating away.

Smoke and dust high up there,
Flying right through the air.
See the red blood in the hot mud,
Swords and boards scratching where,
People fighting everywhere.

Hear the sound the fire makes,
Whooshing through the fiery gates.
Wild horses gathering where,
People lying dead everywhere.
See the ground cracking through,
Lava boiling, hot stew.

People running through the doors,
People striking with their swords.
Oh help! Oh help! People cry,
Oh little town of Dublin die.

Gamze Yildirim (10)
Larkman Middle School

PUTTING MYSELF IN THE PICTURE
(Neighbours by Gerry Keon)

I feel my brother opening the door
The doorstep feels cold but I
Feel comfortable with my cat
I feel as if I have done something wrong
With my neighbours looking at me
I see a ball in my front garden
I see another cat on the wall
And I think my cat likes it
I don't think my neighbours are
Talking about the cat on the wall
I hear the cats purring and
Footsteps passing my gate
I feel as if I were touching one of
Those furry mats when I am
Stroking my cat
I had a thought which was
Putting myself as my brother
Playing football and
Having a skinhead
I am feeling tired
I like the way my pink T-shirt
Matches my shoes
I like my neighbour's jewellery
Because it is gold
I would like to know
Why the two old people next door
Are so red
I feel as if I'm in
A world of my own.

Leanne Marvin (11)
Larkman Middle School

PUTTING MYSELF IN SOMEONE ELSE'S PORTRAIT
*(From a portrait of Don Manuel Osorio Manrique de Zuniga
by Goya)*

My name is Manuel
I'm 7 years old
and I'm going to die.
So I'm having my last portrait
done for my mum and dad
to remember me by.
I think my pets will miss me;
I think Jesse will be
saddest of all because
I've had her since I was two
when I found her
abandoned in an alley.
Jesse is scared of people
because she got
stoned by brutal strangers.
I am in my best clothes,
and inside me I wish
mum and dad would stop
fussing over me and
let me do what I want to do.
I've got no friends
apart from my pets,
as I'm rich; I can't play
outside with the other kids.
My house is like
a prison to me.
My house is shadowy
the only bright thing
in it is me.

Daniel Paul Brock (11)
Larkman Middle School

THE MAN WITH THE BIRD

I'm an old man
I'm watching the sun go
down and the dark blue
sky is turning black
a bird from the sky
sat on my finger
he is my friend
and so is my dog
on the floor
his name is Arthur
he is very friendly
I sat and looked all
day and night at the sky
I fell asleep
the birds woke me up
I went inside and had
a cup of tea and some breakfast
I put some music on and
listened to the birds singing
it sounded beautiful.

Sadie Tarragan (11)
Larkman Middle School

PUTTING MYSELF IN THE PICTURE
(Street Kids, Port Glasgow)

My name is Matilda
I love to read
I'm reading a book now
It's called
The Intergalactic Kitchen
I am with two boys
Their names are Shaun and Kim
I am wearing an old jumper
I am sitting on a cold step
We are wearing shorts
Although it is winter
And we are cold
Shaun has an apple
I say 'Can I have a piece?'
And he says 'Yes.'

Toni O'Sullivan (11)
Larkman Middle School

I Love The Smell Of Fresh Cut Grass

I love the smell of fresh cut grass
It is so shiny, it looks like glass.
The smell is so fresh and clean
It reminds me of the polish, Mr Sheen.
The look of the grass looks so nice
It reminds me of fresh cold ice.
When the grass dies the smell goes away
But it has been there from the very first day.
When it comes back next spring
That same old smell makes me grin.

Amy White (10)
Wensum Middle School

MEETING A DRAGON

The dragon is a fearful beast
He likes to eat us for his feast.
He has a very spiky back
He puts people in its sack.
His skin is a pale green
He really is extremely mean.
The dragon is very huge
He's as mean as Uncle Scrooge.
He really is a mean machine
He keeps his teeth squeaky clean
I thought they came up on telly
Now my legs are shaking like jelly.

Joanna Lawn (9)
Wensum Middle School

MY DOG TOBY

My dog Toby was so cute,
he liked eating biscuits and fruit.

We used to give him a wash in the bath,
but he looked so lovely we had a laugh.

Now Toby is far away,
I think of him every single day.

Sometimes I start crying,
It makes me feel like I'm dying.

I see his face in my mind,
My mind is saying find, find, find.

Zoe Milbank (10)
Wensum Middle School

I WISH

I wish I was a penguin
Swimming through the sea
Like an eagle swooping down
To catch its prey
Like a bird singing to a dove
Like a cat miaowing its love.

Luke Jackson (10)
Wensum Middle School

CHALK

Chalk is like a spotty glass on its side.
Chalk is like a white puffy cloud hanging by
Chalk is like an old man's bedroom
Because it's cold and dusty.
Chalk is like an old white piston.
Chalk is like the Sahara desert all powdery and dry.
Chalk is cold and smooth just like a skeleton's finger.

David Rigby (10)
Wensum Middle School

MY INK CARTRIDGE

It's like a deep blue ocean
It's like boiling water when
I write with it.
It's a blue snake eating a rat
It reminds me of the water measure
On my kettle
It's a short handwriting pen.
It's a bullet ready to shoot the
Information on the paper.

Iain Shelvington (9)
Wensum Middle School

MY SHADOW

My shadow is like a burglar
dressed in black following me about.
My shadow is like a big black
rain cloud up above.
My shadow is like a little black dog
following me everywhere I go.
My shadow is like lots of darkness
the shape as a person.
My shadow is like a blackboard
stuck on the wall.
My shadow is like a big strip
of black wallpaper.

Lisa-Marie Wright (9)
Wensum Middle School

SCISSORS

Standing on their handles
they're like a rocket
ready to take off.
Open they're like
a friendly old man
with a moustache.
Closed they're like
a bird with a long beak.
They're like a sword
with two handles.
They're like a crocodile
with snapping jaws,
ready to bite anything
in its way.
They're like a frozen
silvery stream.

Joanna Goodman (9)
Wensum Middle School

THE CLASSROOM CLOCK

It's like a cylinder after
it has been gone over
with a steamroller, all flat!
It's a giant's wrist watch off its strap.
It's a car wheel on the back
of a jeep, but on the wall instead,
and the red hand is the wheel trim
spinning as the car moves forward.
It's a boiled egg in the morning
after it has been opened.
It looks like a full moon too.

Christopher Carr (10)
Wensum Middle School

IN MY LUNCHBOX

My sandwich is like a bouncy castle because it is soft.
My yoghurt is like a slimy swamp because it is thick.
My crisps are like a flying saucer flying through the air.
My drink is like a swimming pool that is very long and deep.
My chocolate bar is like a skyscraper because it is long and wide.
And my apple is just like a planet very far away.

Thomas Kerin (10)
Wensum Middle School

MY FAMILY

My mum is as busy as a bee
And as lovely as a red red rose.

My dog is as mad as a mad hatter
And as funny as a clown
And as fast as a rocket
As crafty as a wolf
As gold as treacle.

My nanna is as mad as a dog
And as funny as a clown
And as cool as a cat.

Alexa Rae Keely Bush (10)
Wensum Middle School

MY DAY ON THE BEACH

On my day at the beach
I walked along the sand as soft as silk
and the warm sun like a burning ball above me.
The sky was like a huge blue sheet over the earth,
And as the dark blue sea sparkled like sapphires
I decided to take a quick, cool dip.
As I walked along the silky, soft sand
it changed to hard stones as sharp as glass all broken up.
Then I felt the cool sea like ice on my toes,
and I paddled for a bit and I felt like a duck.

Then I walked over for some ice-cream.
I got the money out of my wet pocket,
and it was as cold as carrots.
I got the creamy ice-cream
and sunk my teeth into it.
It was as white as snow and
as creamy as banana cream cake.
Then I stepped in something as slimy as snails
and as slippery as a soapy sink
but it was only a piece of sloppy seaweed.

Jennie Human (10)
Wensum Middle School

MY PENCIL

My pencil is a Pink Panther
and it's yellow like bananas.
It has pink and yellow dots on it
like a dippy Dalmatian.
It is like a giraffe's neck.
It reminds me of blackberries.
The rubber is like a sponge.

Kaylea Leggett (9)
Wensum Middle School

THROUGH THAT DOOR

Through that door
Is a river flowing into the sea
On the beach big waves splash
Pebbles roll towards the sea
The sun is shining brightly
People swim in the water
A beachball rolls into the sea
A little boy cries.

Carla Moore (8)
Wensum Middle School

THROUGH THAT DOOR

Through that door
Is wildlife and a river
If you jump in
It will make you shiver
Furry rabbits and cute squirrels
Scurrying by
In the river is fish and ducks
Waiting for you.

Liessa Moy (8)
Wensum Middle School

THROUGH THAT DOOR

Through that door
Is a lovely land of sweets
You could eat them all
And you wouldn't get full
Can you see all the shapes?
They're made of Chocolate Buttons
The cars are made of squishy marshmallow
You would like to live there!

Roisin Fenlon (9)
Wensum Middle School

THROUGH THAT DOOR

Through that door
Is a jungle
A harmony of peacefulness
Bright sun, lovely breeze
Blowing from side to side
No one is as tall as the big tree
Can you hear the kookaburra bird?
Is it a dream or not?

Katrina Berry (9)
Wensum Middle School

THROUGH THAT DOOR

Through that door
Is the big huge universe
Endless space
For you to find an alien race.
There is a place called Earth
Moving from the sun.
There's lots of black holes
And comets' tails like poles.

Mitchell Hill (8)
Wensum Middle School

THROUGH THAT DOOR

Through that door
Is a garden of sweets
A pond full of Coke with bubblegum fish
And a wall of Jelly Babies laying on each other
The lawn is chocolate ready to be eaten
And candy trees so you can chew for ever and ever
Marshmallow flowers for my dad
And Smarties weeds to pick and eat.

Joel Fiddy (8)
Wensum Middle School

THROUGH THAT DOOR

Through that door
Is a model
Sitting in a red room.
She looks lovely
In her flowing dress.
It is a romantic scene.
A lovely scent of perfume
And relaxing music playing.

Gemma Howes (8)
Wensum Middle School

THROUGH THAT DOOR

Through that door
Is a world of Cyber Pets
They beep as they craze
They like to play for hours
They are small squares on screens
Lively with cheeky faces
Each has buttons to press
They die but they come back to life.

Adam Tacon (9)
Wensum Middle School

IMAGINATION

I should like to paint the wind
on the sun in the middle of the night.
I should like to hear the scent
of a butterfly in the jungle.
I should like to touch the roar
of a tiger as it pounces on its prey.
I should like to take home a rainbow
so that I can keep its colours for ever.

Lisa Bush (8)
White Woman Lane Middle School

I WISH

I wish I could see God in Heaven,
see the sunset rise
and see a tooth fairy collecting my tooth.

I wish I could hear my feet
sink into the sand on a sunny day
and hear the flowers open against my ear
when the wind isn't blowing.

Jaye Valori (8)
White Woman Lane Middle School

I SHOULD LIKE TO . . .

I should like to paint the cry of
an ant flying in space.
I should like to hear the breath of
a fire hose in the Sahara desert.
I should like to touch the heartbeat of
a unicorn's horn on the end of a pencil.
I should like to paint the morning's air
under the sea.
I should like to hear the footsteps
of a woodlouse on Mars.
I should like to touch the heart
of a portrait in a blue whale's eye.
I should like to take home the
voice of a CD-ROM on the moon.

Jonathan Bliss (8)
White Woman Lane Middle School

I SHOULD LIKE TO . . .

I should like to paint the sound of
the sea on a sunny day.
I should like to hear the Earth
spinning round in space.
I should like to touch a mirage
of a waterfall in the desert.
I should like to take home a ring
of Saturn from the solar system.

I should like to paint the sound
of a plane going through the clouds
on a windy day.
I should like to hear the smell of
a fish on a cold winter night.
I should like to touch the sound of
an owl hooting on a dark night.
I should like to take home the
sound of the wind from the Antarctic ocean.

Stuart Feek (9)
White Woman Lane Middle School

I SHOULD LIKE TO . . .

I should like to paint the air in
the middle of the Red Sea.
I should like to hear the icicles in the
middle of the Sahara Desert.
I should like to touch the moon under the sea.
I should like to take home the Galaxy
on a cold winter's night.

Lisa Mehran (8)
White Woman Lane Middle School

I Should Like To . . .

I should like to paint the electricity in
a lightbulb.
I should like to hear the heartbeat
in the sea on the moon.
I should like to touch an electric eel
on a freezing cold Arctic night.
I should like to take home a cloud
on the boiling sun.
I should like to paint the sound
of the Solar System travelling through space.
I should like to hear the smell of a star
during the day.
I should like to touch a Stingray
in the scorching summer's sun.
I should like to take home the
Sizzling summer's sun on top of Mars.

Liam Jermy (8)
White Woman Lane Middle School

I Should Like To . . .

I should like to paint thin air on a summer day.
I should like to hear a flower growing on a summer day.
I should like to touch the sun on a summer day.
I should like to take home a wild cat on a summer day.
I should like to plant the stars singing on a summer night.
I should like to hear thin air when it is singing on a summer day.
I should like to touch a ghost sleeping on a winter night.
I should like to take home a chocolate mountain.

Kylie Franklin (9)
White Woman Lane Middle School

I SHOULD LIKE TO . . .

I should like to paint a robin's song
on a cold day.

I should like to hear the stars
twinkling in the sky.

I should like to touch the beat
of a butterfly's wings.

I should like to take home the sun
and put it on my shelf.

Lucy Ann Blythe (9)
White Woman Lane Middle School

I SHOULD LIKE TO . . .

I should like to paint the air
on the moon when it is light.
I should like to hear a volcano
in the dead sea.
I should like to touch the Atlantis city
when it rose onto land again.
I should like to take home the rainforest
swaying gently in the summer wind.

I should like to paint the sound
of a civil war in May.
I should like to hear a lioness
on Mars in the winter wind.
I should like to touch a caveman
in the winter of the Stone Age.
I should like to take home a dinosaur
in the Stone Age.

Laura Chaplin (8)
White Woman Lane Middle School

I SHOULD LIKE TO . . .

I should like to paint the weight of air in a historic sea
I should like to hear a speck of dust flying around the stars
I should like to touch the air in space
I should like to take home the mind of the sea.

I should like to paint the roar of a lion in the forest
I should like to hear the wind on a still day
I should like to touch the song of a robin on a summer's day
I should like to take home the moon out of space.

Ben Peirson (9)
White Woman Lane Middle School

I SHOULD LIKE TO..

I should like to paint
a whale in the sea.

I should like to hear a
monkey in a forest.

I should like to touch a
shark in the sea.

I should like to take
home a polar bear.

Jonathan Miller (9)
White Woman Lane Middle School

I WISH

I wish I could hear a dog miaow.
I wish I could hear bluebells ring.
I wish the moon was made out of cheese.
I wish I could kick my best friend to the moon.
I wish I could see my grandad turn into an orang-utan.
I wish I could hear Shaun *baa*.

Lindsey Kemp (8)
White Woman Lane Middle School

I WISH

I wish I could hear the crack of dawn
and the bluebell rise
I wish I could hear a lizard
creeping along the creaking floorboards
and a dinosaur roaring at my face
I wish I could see the sun rise
and a baby lizard break out of its egg.

Donna Bloomfield (8)
White Woman Lane Middle School

I WISH

I wish I could see Heaven and see my dog,
cat and hamster.

I wish I could hear my dog in Heaven.

I wish I could hear the leopard as it creeps
through the grass.

I wish I could feel a toucan's beak.

I wish I could feel my dog again.

I wish I could have a good tame tiger.

Charlotte Pollard (8)
White Woman Lane Middle School

I WISH

I wish I could see King George fight the dragon
behind a tree.

I wish I could hear a T-Rex on his head.

I wish I could be a T-Rex.

I wish I could have a little pet dragon
which would not kill me.

I wish I could smell the moon from earth.

I could go back to 1861.

George Beacock (8)
White Woman Lane Middle School

I WISH

I wish I could see my dad at work
I wish I could see my rabbit in heaven
I wish I could see my nanny in heaven
I wish I could plant a seed of love in my heart
I wish I could be in heaven and see what is in there.

Lucy Mocklow (8)
White Woman Lane Middle School

I WISH

I wish I could see the waves crashing against the rocks.
I wish I could hear the whole wide world.
I wish that my sister would treat me good.
I wish that I could go through the rainforest
while it's pouring with rain.
I wish that I could ride on a shooting star.
I wish that I had all the animals I wanted.

Anna Brunton (8)
White Woman Lane Middle School

I WISH

I wish I could see a dinosaur.
I wish I could hear the crack of dawn.
I wish I could have the desert in my room.
I wish I could sit on a fluffy white cloud.
I wish I could hear the snow floating to the ground.
I wish I could be a tiger.

Stephen Ryan (8)
White Woman Lane Middle School

I WISH

I wish I could see the colours of sunset from a bird's view.
I wish I could hear the fish think.
I wish I could hear the fish eat all day.
I wish I could see a chimpanzee playing.

Shelley Gunning (9)
White Woman Lane Middle School

I WISH

I wish I could see a rainbow from a bird's view.
I wish I could see a sloth.
I wish I could hear God speaking to my guinea-pig.
I wish I could feel the sky.
I wish I could play with a bird.
I wish I was a baby again.

Lauren Cook (8)
White Woman Lane Middle School

I Wish

I wish I could see the sun setting in the sky,
colours spreading around and around the sun.

I wish I could hear the dolphins crying in the ocean.

I wish I could feel the roughness of the bare trees
in the winter.

I wish I could hear my footsteps in the leaves
scrunching up.

I wish I could be on the moon eating cheese.

I Wish I could be a superstar in Hollywood,
lights everywhere.

Jenna Myers (9)
White Woman Lane Middle School

I WISH

I wish I could hear my animals in heaven.
I wish I could see the rainforest.
I wish I could feel a leopard, a soft baby leopard
and Mummy.
I wish I could be a baby again.
I wish I could be an animal.
I wish I could see a sloth hanging on a tree.

Sinead Bird (8)
White Woman Lane Middle School

I Wish

I wish I could hear my dad snoring at night
I wish I was famous
I wish I could feel the stars
I wish I could feel a twister in the rain
I wish I could feel a tornado
I wish I could make money.

Jamie Marrison (8)
White Woman Lane Middle School

I WISH

I wish I could hear a spider scream
when I trap it in the door

I wish I could see my eyes
I wish I could see my Dad at work

I wish I could feel the wind
rushing by my face

I wish I could feel the rough sea
I wish I could feel that I can fly.

Sam Atkins (9)
White Woman Lane Middle School

I WISH

I wish I could see a Viking ship.
I wish I could hear the crackling of a baby bird's egg.
I wish I could feel the sky.
I wish I could be a bird.
I wish I could feel a life of a flower.
I wish I could see a desert.
I wish I could be at home.

Kirsty Gray (8)
White Woman Lane Middle School

WINTER

Winter is ice dust and grains of rice, all painted snowy white.
Spines from a porcupine are those frosted blades of grass.
The post boxes mutate to proud snowmen
Whilst the king of the cold nips your frozen hands.
It's the breath of the wind, mighty and strong.
The warriors of winter are drawing near.
The war of winter begins.
The king of cold takes on the beast of the wind.
The sky erupts and the booming begins.
The cold pokes all living things with its freezing spear.
But the beast fights back and its roaring brings fear.
Then their time has gone and winter is no more.
The spring is here and peace is now restored.

Adam Dyble (11)
Woodland View Middle School

THE REVENGE OF THE ROBOTIC ANT

The beautiful robot hovering above the city,
Demolishing all the buildings,
Terrifying all the people.
The chequered, mysterious, indestructible
robot destroying all the land,
Shooting lasers everywhere,
Waiting for it to leave,
Trying to blow it up,
The huge dangerous machine.

Joe West (10)
Woodland View Middle School

ALIEN INVASION

Something invading our world,
Something out of the blue,
Turning the sky from blue to
Yellows, oranges and reds,
Something chequered,
Something indestructible,
Wants revenge,
Burning buildings to the ground.
Ripping,
Tearing,
Destroying our world,
Peace has gone,
Disturbance has struck,
Buildings falling,
People dying,
They are winning,
We are losing,
We are gonna die,
They are gonna live,
People screaming,
People dying,
Aliens taking over our world,
Blowing up our houses.

Stephen Armes (9)
Woodland View Middle School

WINTER

The winter awakes!
His windy breath blows every leaf off every tree.
His sharp icicle claws freeze every housetop,
His cold icy tears lie thick on the ground.
The drips of his saliva fall heavy on the ground, as they
make puddles.
In his anger he crashes down electric beams of light.
With all his strength and power he tries to dominate the world.
He rules the Arctic with his coldness.
He shows no mercy to any living thing.
Then the winds stop and his tears no longer fall.
Everything is subdued.
The sun is born!

Matthew Field (12)
Woodland View Middle School

A WINTER POEM

Winter is a polar bear
His raging anger is the snow
He twirls round like a tornado
He devours everything he finds and leaves
it behind covered in icy snow.

His freezing claws leave their mark and
turn to ice on the paths.
His wet icy breath
leaves patterns on car windows
and buildings.

His tears fall and melt the snow
that is settled on the ground.
Drool falls off his deadly teeth and turns to
hail that plunges to Earth.
His domain is the Arctic where he rules
in great pride.
Now everything is silenced and he is gone.

Andrew Loveday (11)
Woodland View Middle School

WINTER

Winter spreads his cold breath across the ground.
His breath, the frost spread everywhere,
His tears, the snow falling from the sky,
His anger, the storms clouding the sky
As he unleashes his power over the land.
The world freezes over as he shows us his might.
He wrecks houses, he spreads his cold,
He enjoys making people suffer -
It's his job and he does it well.
He shoves cars and lorries from the road,
He pushes people from the paths.
He moves in every year and makes us
Dread going out of doors.
He'll freeze us then push us away like dolls.
He stays for three or four months
And then spring knocks *him* away.

Nicholas Shorten (11)
Woodland View Middle School

THE MONSTER FROM MARS

If you saw it
You would say it's
Horrifying
Shocking
You would say it comes from Mars
Only if you saw it.

If you saw it
You would say it's
Mysterious
Petrifying
Gigantic
You would say it comes from Mars
Only if you saw it.

If you saw it
you would say it's
Revolting
Hideous
You would say it comes from Mars
Only if you saw it
Oh yes only if you saw it.

Adam Skinner (10)
Woodland View Middle School

FIREWORKS

Sudden sparks in the skies
As if God has spilt glitter
From his heavenly den.
The colours are magnificent -
Red, orange and blue.
To think every other night
All we see is black
Like dark black coal.
Everything now lit up
Like the first break of dawn.
I feel so full of joy
Just sitting with my family
On this magical night.
Everything so glittery
Orange, purple and silvery.
The purple is a geranium
Opening in the sky,
The blue is the clear skies
On a summer's day,
The red is the dancing flame
In the fire before me,
The yellow is a flickering flame
Dancing in the night-time breeze
And finally the silver
A tear from my eye, the dewy grass,
A silver spoon or broken glass,
A tiara upon a princess' head,
The shining grin of a skeleton lying down dead!
So that's the end of Bonfire night
As the sky is filled with a beautiful light.

Jason Postle (11)
Woodland View Middle School

PATTERNS OF NIGHT

The sky is a black blanket, bringing the sun to rest.
The dancing flames are tiny red imps, cackling and spitting in
the night.

The rockets are gliding white as chalk snakes,
Leaping to the specks of silver and dying into coloured glitter.

The car lamps are gleaming eyes of the deadly coal-black cat.
The moon is a silver tossed coin in the black sea.

The exploding jumping-jack is a silver lion pouncing on its
invisible prey.
The screaming rocket is the screech of the parrot as it explodes
into a thousand feathers of light.

The randomly rainbow-coloured crackler firework shoots up,
exploding into a million gunshots.
The Catherine wheel is a rainbow arm swinging at the smoky air.

The sparklers are the white snapping jaws of the black stick-snake.
The traffic light firework is a champagne bottle just uncorked.

Blue is the rope that barricades us from the dancing array of flowers,
Brown are the posts we lean on when watching the beautiful display.

Rebecca Rushton (10)
Woodland View Middle School

ANIMALS AT HOME

At the bottom of the garden,
In a shed all of their own,
We have five fat chickens,
Three white, one black, one brown.
They lay fresh eggs every day,
Sometimes in their nest,
But often we have to look,
In the hedge for the rest.

We have a dog called Ben,
Pedigree unknown.
He's like a walking hearth rug,
And he likes to chew a bone.
He doesn't come when you call him now,
He's going a bit deaf you see,
But we have lots of fun,
My friend Ben and me.

My sister brought home two goats one day,
By new year there were three,
Rosie, Gemma and Holly were their names,
A handful you would agree.
They ate everything they shouldn't,

But mostly liked carrots and hay,
Sadly they had to leave,
And left for junior farm one day.

Lee Bryant (12)
Woodland View Middle School

THE CHARMER

A silent creature creeps along,
He knows the path, he can't go wrong.
This journey home, many times he has made,
If something comes he will hide in the shade.
Along the beaten track he goes,
Where he is no one else knows.
Then something makes him turn his head,
He stops in his tracks, stops dead.
A human playing music, beyond the trees,
He can hear clearly because of the breeze.
He changed his way, turns to the right,
Then he is out, in the light.
He is exposed but he doesn't care,
He doesn't even turn a hair.
The music is entrancing, he can't keep away,
He stays there all night and soon it is day.
He knows he must go, he really should,
But he would stay a while longer, if he could.

Abby Lake (10)
Woodland View Middle School

THE STORM

Crash, clash,
The thunder roars,
Slam, boom,
Flash, crackle,
Zeus's lightning bolts aimed,
Swish, blow,
Another tree under his power,
Twisting, turning,
His anger displayed,
Rip, rumble,
Wrenching tiles' frenzied destroying,
He tears at everything within his reach,
A wild thing.

Whisper, whisper,
No reason given - it calms.

Then splash, splosh,
Filling up ditches and ponds with his tears,
Swish, cackle,
Enveloping the world with Hades' cloak,
Drip, drop,
Rain stops,
Shine, gleam,
Sun rises,
Her rays illuminate,
Quiet, rumble,
The storm quells,
Ire assuaged.

Imogen Maureen Clayton (11)
Woodland View Middle School

THE SNOW LEOPARD

The shy snow leopard camouflaging well,
In the white, white snow as cold as hell.
Crouching low in the Mongolian hills,
There's a man approaching with a gun that kills.
The rare animal blends in the snow.
But, its eyes seem to give a glow,
Like jewels in the snow.

The man noticed the eyes in a trice,
Among the slippery slush and ice.
The gun was poised, the bullet was ready,
To shoot the creature ready, steady . . .
There was a *bang!* but the leopard leapt,
What disaster it would be if the leopard
had slept!

For, with one big shot, he would be dead,
If he had slept to rest his head.
Running like wind it ran a mile,
'Cause the man's gun shot with style
at the creature's head.
This leopard here is nowhere to be seen,
Only flat on the floor, for that man was so mean.

Jodie Leate (12)
Woodland View Middle School

THE SHELL

Outside the shell
Were once rough edges
But now beaten smooth by rocks.
A misty grey shell,
Ridges filled with a few grains of sand
That were caught when the tide came in.
A piece of seaweed was caught under the bottom.
Inside the shell,
A strange, salty smell,
A barnacle on the wall
The sea trickled in under the shell,
And the barnacle snapped.
Under the shell,
A pale pink,
A little wet, a little sandy,
But as smooth as glass.
it dreams away many a summer day,
Seagulls calling above,
A water-logged dog barking and jumping.
If I give the shell away, certainly I shall miss it,
Its misty colour, the barnacle beneath,
Without my hands to feel it and keep it in its secret place
under the broken sea defence where the water collects.
My secret place, my secret shell,
By the cliffs.

Danielle Sempers (11)
Woodland View Middle School

WINTER

Winter's arrived,
Its strong breath sweeps the trees,
Its anger breaks as the lightning strikes across the midnight sky.
In the morning he falls asleep, as the grey clouds cover him,
But as he rises at nightfall, his envy continues,
As his tears of anger hit the ground with a thump,
He spreads his evil coldness around, killing trees,
Forcing people into warmer clothes and putting
animals into hibernation.
As he storms through the country he shows no mercy.
His frightening has no end.
When he sneezes, cold icicles of snow fall down
covering the ground like a bedsheet,
But as the February month comes,
Winter fades and joyous spring appears.

Marc Fuller (12)
Woodland View Middle School

HOW MYSTERIOUS

An angry mysterious monster,
Being controlled by man,
Comes down from a different, horrible
space than we know,
It's black, blue and white,
With a dangerous claw to crush
building down,
coming down from a rocky
opaque land up in the sky,
It is immortal, revolting
and gigantic as a claw crushes
a building,
Tearing off the roof,
How spooky!

Katie Lewis (10)
Woodland View Middle School